the mundane

POEMS BY
MELISSA ELDER

SECOND EDITION

ISBN: (hardcover edition) 9798987477083
ISBN: (soft binding edition) 9798987477090
Cover Design: Achsa Phillippi
Editing and layout design: K.J Wetherholt
Publishing Rights: M&B Books LLC, KJ Wetherholt
Cover art and sketches by Susanna Maria Hackett / I Love You More Than Any Number, LLC.
For further information, please contact: susannemaria@iloveyoumorethananynumber.com
All artwork is used in this book by agreement.

Dedicated to
those who are knee deep in
the mundane.

Authors Note

To rhyme or not to rhyme. I like when poems rhyme. I like when I can understand them. But while reading poems from the Greats, the ones that shaped the world, I question my abilities and I'm left to wonder. Such as these in life do we compare.

poems

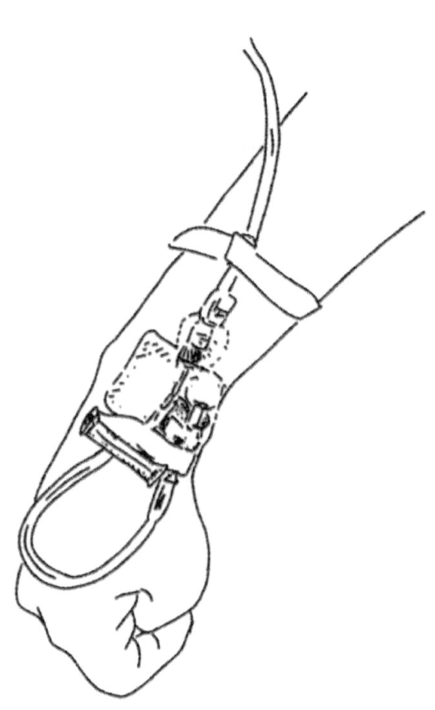

Labor

She was mangled and sweated,
her breath sharp and desperate.
Her hair was a nest of mess.

Her muscles sore
and body broken.

But her eyes told a different story.
One of longing.
Of wanting,
waiting,
of
loving.

Birth

Her face was soft. So soft.
Cheeks flushed and pink.
Around her eyes, a calming contentment.
Her smile tired and reserved,
she looked at home.

How can someone look so peaceful?

In her arms,
a wrapped
sleeping baby.

The smell

When they're born, they have a smell-
unlike anything else.

Heaven still lingering maybe.

Hold after hold
kiss after kiss
hug after hug
cuddle after cuddle

their smell fades.

They start to smell like us.

That's how we know their smell can no
longer remind them of heaven.

The heavenly smell has faded,
life begins.

Surrendering my heart

My child.
My child, I surrender my heart to you.

It's no longer mine to toy with.
It's no longer mine to conspire with-
to live with.

My heart belongs to you now.
From the moment I heard yours come alive.

So please. I beg you please,

hold it gently.

What they don't tell you

I never in a million years
could have imagined
my bad days
consisting of
checking my child's diaper
in front of other people-
only to find poop
on my finger.

It goes fast

"It goes by so fast",
They always seem to say.
"Savor every minute!"
While they go on their merry way.

Back to their homes,
so quiet and so clean.
No dishes in the sink
no toddlers to be seen.

I just stand there,
my kids running wild.
Exhaustion in my bones,
holding a screaming child.

"But I'm so tired!!"
I want to yell at them.
"You just can't remember
What it was like back then."

The bags under my eyes
Start to hang so deep.
I haven't brushed my hair
I haven't brushed my teeth.

Will this ever end?
The constant sleepless nights?
Endless dirty diapers
or sibling screams and fights?

And then right there,
as I'm knee deep in stress,
I hear my daughter ask
with flowers on her dress.

"Can I help you mom,
With anything you need?"
Her face so warm and kind
in her voice I hear the plead.

It stops me in my tracks,
I can't help but sit and stare.
"When did she grow up?
When did she start to care?"

And that's when I realize
that time does go by fast.
How do I savor this moment?
How do I make it last?

I stop everything I'm doing
and get down on one knee.
I hold her to my chest,
let myself just be.

I'll savor this minute.
I'll smell her hair.
I'll study her features.
I'll hold her near.

Split

Am I my child's
biggest bully?

Or my child's
greatest advocate?

Sometimes
it's hard
to tell.

Jekyll and Hyde

I slowly open the door and see her standing in her crib.
Patiently waiting for me to pick her up.
She's smiling all over her face.
Giggling even.
I feel giddy to hold her.
I can't wait to hold her.
I giggle too.
I realize how much I missed her while she napped.
I pick her up and put my cheek next to her soft, red, post-nap cheek.
I can't get close enough to her skin.
I ask her for a kiss with her cheeks so soft and red.
She leans in and gives me a kiss so obediently.

I melt. I die. I might even cry.
She's perfect.

I take her downstairs with a skip in my step.
I put her down.
She points to something and makes a sound.
"What is it you want baby girl?"
I point to things to see if she'll nod.
No nod.
She starts to scream.
Reaching and pointing.
I try more earnestly to grab what she's wanting.
Nothing.
No satisfaction.
I start to panic.
"This? Do you want this?" I start to beg.
My voice with visible desperation.
Her voice is getting louder.
Her yells turn to screams.
Loud shrieks of agony that hurt my ears.
I pick her up.
She slaps me and screams.
Now I'm angry.

She starts to cry.
I feel aggressive.
Her screams are loud and her cries are fierce.
She's slapping things around her.
Anger has taken over us both.
Now screaming and slapping.
I'm frantic beyond rational thinking.

I hand her a cracker that was on the counter.

Silence.
She is silent.
Happily wiping away her tears.

I sigh with relief, and think

When the devil is her next nap?

Kisses

I have her on my side,
while doing my daily chores.
Along for the ride,
as I'm sweeping these floors.

She makes a little coo,
I look at her plump lips
I need her kiss bad,
as she's propped up on my hips.

I ask her for kisses,
she looks me in my eye
cups my face in her hands,
her mouth opens wide.

Our faces come together
with my lips puckered out.
Her kiss a bit wet,
milky drool, I have no doubt.

Although it was sloppy,
Improved only with time,
it's the highlight of my day,
to feel her lips on mine.

Home

For what is a home?

A mere place
to rest my heart.

It need not be
anything fancier.

Unlearning

One thing
I've learned
from adulthood

is the need to
unlearn most things
from childhood.

"What do you do?"

"What do you do all day?"
He asked with his slicked back hair,
black tailored suit-
grinning condescendingly.

I looked down at my sweats.
My hair slicked back in grease.

My pride in flames.

I paused for a moment, what do I do all day?
Me, a stay-at-home mom by choice.

I thought about waking my girls up with a kiss
making new recipes
hot showers
reading a book
walking in the mountains, my baby strapped to my chest
lighting living room candles
playing the piano
noon day sex
discovering new parks
sledding
being lazy
being productive
fall leaves crunching
laughing with my friends
trying new restaurants
planting spring flowers
dancing in the kitchen
opening the curtains
writing poetry

I look up at the man,
while grinning condescendingly-

"I do whatever I want."

Motherhood is not

Motherhood
is not a duty
it is not oppression
it is not an obligation
it is not soul sucking
it is not an identity
it is not a must.

It is simply a choice,
and one where beauty can be found.

A rose

The rose,
much like the woman.

So velvety.
So stunning.
A vision to behold.

Try and hold her down
and she'll make you bleed.

Doing it

"It doesn't take much,"
the ignorant might sigh,
unaware of the pain,
because they've never dared to try.

It doesn't take much?
Just a daily sacrifice.
Running for my life,
and not thinking twice.

Dedicating every minute,
pushing myself every mile.
Constant sweat on my brow,
shoving down all the bile.

It doesn't take much?
To train all day?
Bruising my weary bones,
aches that don't go away.

Repeating all the mantras
I've memorized by heart.
Get me past another minute,
further from the start.

So, to you it may not seem like much,
for all you see are the smiles.
But inside I'm fighting desperately
to run these endless miles.

All they see

I have to laugh at those people
who look at parenthood and only see

stinky diapers
loud screams
boogers
messy hair
fighting
dirt
scrapes
late nights
crying
sore nipples
stretch marks
wrinkles
weight gain
hitting
chasing
yelling
sighing
no free time
screen time
early mornings
exhaustion

Because they're dead right.
Except for the part where
love overrides it all.

What is love

"Mom what is love?"
She so innocently asked.
I sat and thought about this
while finishing up my task.

She asked me again,
my face in a stare.
How can I answer
how much that word bares.

How can I answer
that it's out of my control.
The love I feel for her
overtakes `my entire` soul.

Or when I look at her sister
a wrapped gift from God.
A perfect child freely given
to a mother so flawed.

Or when I look at dad
I don't just see a man.
My life to him I've given,
my body, my heart, my hand.

I look down at her
as she patiently waits.
I want to tell her everything
but for now, all I can say

is that "love is simple.
It's a feeling from inside.
You'll know when you feel it.
The smiles are hard to hide."

She looks down from me
and I can hear her mind go.

And just like that
I see the smile start to grow.

"Oh, I see" she says
"I know exactly what love is.
Love is when I help my sister,
and she gives me a kiss."

What love is to me:

Love to me,
is saving the best parts
of my personality
for the people
who matter
the most.

The struggle,
is to decipher the people
in my daily life,
who matter
the most

and love them.

Staring out the window

"What's the point?" She thought
as she sat and stared
out the window in her kitchen,
the city lights flared.

Everything I do,
gets forgotten anyways.
Everything I accomplish
will get zero praise.

It seems as though
the days are all for naught.
Everyone moves on,
and I'll be forgot.

Why do I bother
with these menial things?
These tiny little chores
that add up to nothing.

I want to be someone
I want to soar
I don't want to be forgotten
I want to be more.

But how can I do so
with this life so mundane?
How can I escape
this never-ending train?

Then I feel a tug
on my shirt from behind.
Startled from my thoughts
her soft blue eyes I find.

The reason I do it,
the reminder to why I stay-
her needing me now
gets me through another day.

When it's quiet

What do you think about
when all is quiet?
Where does
the heart roam?

What parts from your past
come up fast?
What memories
take you back home?

When the music is off,
your phone is away-
what comes to the surface
of your mind?

When you're left alone
no one else-
who are you?
Who would we find?

Precious

I've noticed as I get older,
I use words such as "precious" and "tender"
or "beautiful" and "unbelievable."
Words that I thought as a child,
were only used by the old.

I understand now.

I understand how precious time really is,
how tender a child can be.
Or how beautiful a heart can shine.

I understand now, the unbelievable truth,
this life is to be savored.

Infertility

Infertility
is like not getting an
invite to the best party
in the world-
that you were told
you were supposed
to go to.

Agony

Where a mother's love
is planted
at their birth, equal
is her
agony
planted
at their death.

Nothing in vain

I'm imagining for one moment
that every single experience
I've ever had
in my life
up to this point in time,
has been for the soul purpose
of helping someone else.

What does it mean to be a good person?

I look around my home,
wondering,
to be a good person
would I have to sell everything-
giving the money to those who
need it more than I do?

Or does it mean
to simply be grateful
for the things
I have-
needing them or not?

The little devil may tempt

Is it possible to have everything?
I ask the devil on my shoulder.
He responds quickly with a "yes."

He mentions
the things that I long for;
the money, the house, the dress.

I feel envious
these people I know
that have everything he has said.

My greed gets deeper,
my desire gets stronger,
my eyes now only see red.

Then - out of nowhere
my shoulder angel whispers,
"My dear, you have everything already".

"You have girls who giggle,
a home so warm,
a husband whose love is steady."

An image of my girls
come quickly to my mind,
each of them laying by my side.

One of them laughing
while the other one jokes,
the thought makes me smile so wide.

Another thought comes
just as quickly as the other,
of my husband rubbing my back.

that I've had
a very long day -
he's kindly trying to help me relax.

Now I'm sitting so still,
thinking all that I have,
smiling, as I reminisce.

I'm feeling ever so grateful
For all I've been given
wishing everyone can feel like this.

Dark corners

I have poison lodged
in the darkest corners of my heart.
It lingers
and it simmers.
I can feel it.

How do I rid this tar
from my heart?
I want to live.
I want to thrive.

I don't want these shadows
robbing me from the happiness
to be had in my day.

This isn't who I want to be.
This isn't how I want to live.

Quiet, simple prayers

My dearest Heavenly Father,

thank you for my beautiful family.

The very reason for which I live.
The very reason for which I exist.

I love them.
Oh, my goodness, I love them.

Please let me keep them forever.

And sorry for yelling at them today.

Gracefully aging

At first, I notice the age spots,
then the wrinkles start to set in.
I sit and try to remember
what I actually looked like back then.

Face smooth as glass,
muscles visible on my arms.
Abs pulled in tight,
my body nothing but youthful charms.

I don't recognize this body
that I'm staring at now.
I don't even know when it changed
I don't even know how.

I look down at my stomach
stripes, blotches and sags.
I shake my head in disbelief.
I have nothing left to brag.

I look back at my face,
lines deep in my eyes to my hair.
Cheek bones starting to droop just a bit,
I start to wonder if I ever cared.

I think of all the laughs I've had
every single day.
To make these lines so visible,
to make them want to stay.

I think of my babies first home,
as I touch my battle worn torso.
I think of carrying them so close to my heart,
I think back to feeling them grow.

I think about my toes in the sand,
smiling, looking up at the sun.

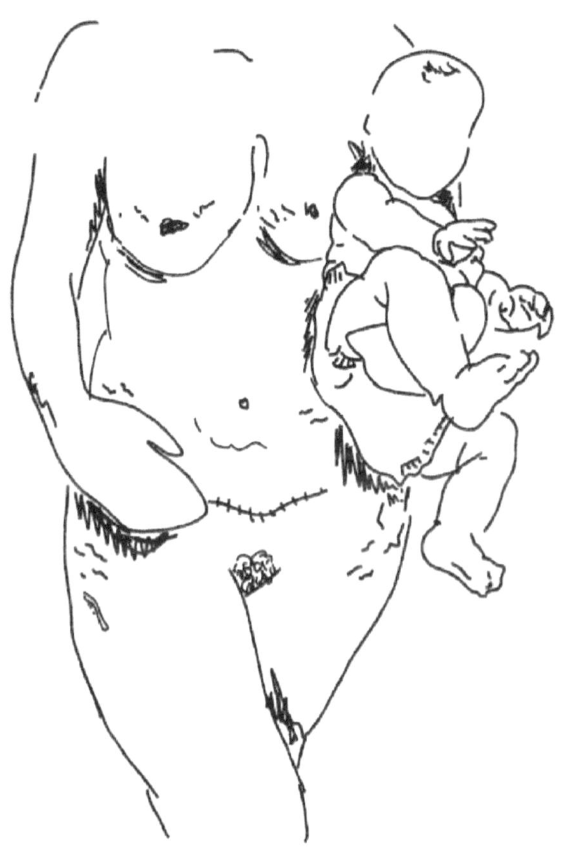

Not caring for the spots on my face being formed
listening to my kids having fun.

I start to smile while looking at this body.
These marks that show my past.
These visible signs that life has been good,
I wouldn't trade them for anything if you asked.

Beauty

It's one thing
to be
naturally beautiful.

It's another thing entirely
for your partner
to make you feel
naturally beautiful-
even though you're not.

Becoming a woman

I've completely lost track
of how many parts
of my body
require shaving
before I can
leave the house.

My body

Most of my life
I have despised,
berated,
critiqued,
shamed,
hated,
made fun of,
blamed,
and mocked
my poor
precious body.

I think
it's about time
I loved it.

Mobile

It's the poison that feeds us.
It's the drug that soothes.
It's the connection that's needed.
It's the distraction that feels.
It's the reason for living.
It's the curse at our children.
It's the start of insecurity.
It's the end to living.
It's the hope that is lost.
It's the smile from a distance.
It's the bond to humanity.
It's the calming in the storm.
It's the guilt in our conscience.
It's the ignorance of rudeness.
It's the trigger for Xanax.
It's the persuasion that's not needed.
It's the need for therapy.
It's the desire to run away.

It's the damn phone.

To serve

It's real nice
to think of someone
and wish them
well.

But it's real love
to be the person
to make them
well.

Believing in God

"Why do you still believe in God?"
She asked.
"Is it not the same as still believing in Santa Claus?"

I thought of these two faith provoking figures.
I thought of the comparisons.

"I guess by choosing to believe
in God there has been more peace in my life.
More happiness.
More positivity.
More love.
More hope.
More joy.
Very much like a child on Christmas,
the happiness is real, believing
in the magic."

Within her a soldier

She didn't know
All that it would take
To prove to herself
That she wouldn't break

No one could hear it
The fight was her own
They couldn't feel the aches
In her mind, heart, and soul

But what they could see
Was a woman to behold
Pushing only herself
To limits untold

They could see a woman
And what she has done
Overcoming herself
Her own battles won

Within her born a soldier
As she pushed and as she cried
For the only reason alone
Was to say at least she tried

A delicate flower

If these tiny
delicate
dainty flowers,
with their petals
near translucent-
can survive the winds
and harsh rains;

then surely,
I can too.

My pride

At first, I deny it happened.
Next, I'll try and blame them.
After that it starts to fester,
I'll feel anger grow within.

I'll turn to every angle,
Until my wrong feels right.
I'll convince whoever I need to
To not give up this fight.

I'll chase after peace all day
I'll run until I cry.
I'll stew into the late hours,
I'll search and wonder why.

I'll easily get upset
For what doesn't go my way.
I'll justify 'til I'm blue in the face
It doesn't matter what you say.

And then just like
that the fight is won.

Peace is felt again.

I feel like I can breathe.
I feel like I am sane.

All because two little words,
"I'm sorry" so simple and pure.
Raw humility is all that's left,
Pride's only lasting cure.

Busy

I never want
to be too busy,
where I can't stop
to notice how
busy others are

and have the time
to help them.

Feminism

Can I still be
a passionate feminist
if I'm a White,
heterosexual,
cisgender,
stay-at-home mom,
with little college education,
who still believes in God?

K, cool.

Having a friend

It's lovely to have a friend.

But its life changing
to have a friend
that feels
like
home.

All for a measly pound

I'll weigh myself.
I'll skip breakfast.
I'll clean harder.
I'll avoid lunches with friends.
I'll avoid holidays.
I'll run until it hurts.
I'll sweat until I'm soaked.
I'll drink myself drown.
I'll weigh myself.

I'll suck in my stomach.
I'll carry all the groceries at once.
I'll flex my butt while driving.
I'll park farther away.
I'll eat as slow as I can.
I'll lose sleep.
I'll compare every limb.
I'll weigh myself.

I'll make a salad.
I'll order another salad.
I'll eat salad after salad after salad.
I'll avoid the mirror.
I'll berate myself in guilt.
I'll exercise while sick.
I'll wake up too early.
I'll covet other bodies.
I'll weigh myself.

I'll think back to what I ate.
I'll think about what I'm going to eat.
I'll take the stairs.
I'll stare at the dessert.
I'll smell the butter and sugar.
I'll pray for restraint.
I'll reset rules.
I'll weigh my food.
I'll weigh myself.

I'll read about tips.
I'll avoid happiness.
I'll write down each bite.
I'll avoid contentment.
I'll set the goals.
I'll avoid satisfaction.
I'll set my alarm.
I'll weigh myself.

I'll do whatever it takes.

To lose that pound.

Wet hair

She walked into
the restaurant with wet hair
and no makeup.
She immediately apologized
for not looking great.

I sat and smiled at her.

I saw a woman
who respected me
enough to be on time.

Who cared more for me
than the way she looked.

I saw a real friend.
And what real beauty looked like.

Real Women

There's nothing more
refreshing
than being surrounded
by women
who remind me
I'm more than
an outfit or a
body size.

A sister

She laughed with her.
She listened to her.
She spent her precious time with her.
And because of that,

life was better.

The people pleaser

She's often fighting
grappling
yearning
and working tirelessly
to please those around her.

The crime is not that
she pleases.
The crime is that she's
unaware of what
pleases her.

Sadness

He's been lingering.
Not close by,
deep down.

But something happens.
Suddenly.
A word. A conversation. A reminder.

He's nearby.
I try to pat him down.
I try to keep him calm.
I try to hide his presence.

But he stays.
He's here.
He's not going away.

I curl up.
I let myself feel him.
I let myself go.
I embrace him.

With the tears that won't stop,
with the flood of everything I feel,
he's relentlessly hovering
over every part of me.

The tears start to calm.
I feel my body lighter
after holding on so tightly.

I feel freed from the sadness
I've kept locked for so long.
I let him go
by giving in.

Conversations with a type 1 diabetic

"My grandpa died of diabetes"
"Does that hurt?"
"I thought you can't eat sugars"
"Is that worth a limb?"
"Are you going low?"
"Why are you tired?"
"My sister died of diabetes"

"Is it hard?"
"Tell me when you're going low"
"You need to stay on top of it"
"Do you need a juice?"
"You probably shouldn't eat that"
"My uncle died of diabetes"

"Are you scared for your kidneys?"
"Think of your girls".
"Are you checking your blood?"
"It can feel like a slow death"
"Everyone's diabetic"
"My mom died of diabetes"

"Thank goodness for medicine"
"That looks hard"
"How is your husband doing with it all?"
"Why do you have so many bruises?"
"Are you going to be, ok?"
"You should warn people when you give yourself a shot"
"My neighbor died of diabetes"

"You seem like you're doing great"
"How many carbs can you have?"
"Is that why it was hard to have kids?"
"Maybe you should check your blood"
"Are you able to still do things?"
"My brother died of diabetes"

"Are you taking care of yourself?"
"Have you seen 'Steel Magnolias'?"
"Are you scared you're going to die?"

Secrets

In life there are secrets.
Secrets that we keep.
Close to our hearts,
Secrets that run deep.

Secrets that we fear
Should never be said.
Out loud on our lips,
Not until we're dead.

But what happens
When vulnerability wins?
When what's escaped?
All that's held within.

Someone sees us,
For who we really are.
Someone sees us
With all our scars.

No excuses to be said
Just standing there bare.
Hoping they won't judge,
Hoping they won't be scared.

But something happens,
completely by surprise.
They see themselves in me,
While looking in my eyes.

They feel compassion,
Empathy starts to grow.
My shame disappears
As their love starts to show.

We connect in ways,
That would have never been possible,

We share the same feelings
And growth feels hopeful.

So why do we keep
these secrets that run deep?
When we are all the same,
You and me.

A lust for humor

You won't win me over
with flowers,
chocolates or gifts.

Bring me to tears
through laughter-
I'll sink right in.

Personality

I have found
the personality
to be the
true face.

Our physical face
has very little to do
with what is ever seen.

Sadly, my make-up bag
tells a different story.

Little devils

I never know if
the little devil on my shoulder
always gets the better
of me,

or if my little angel
just happens to be
as crude as I am.

Experienced

You would think
after so many years
being a human,
I would be somewhat good at it.

Unfortunately, most days,
that's simply
not the case.

Feeling a gust of gratitude

In life there are peaks and valleys.

Most often I feel as if I'm crawling,
hands and knees
through sharp rocks,
reaching for reprieve.

Wading through dark skies,
treacherous valleys,
and noisy canyons-

In hopes to feel the wind on my face.

Arriving at this peak, I know,
I can only go down. I beg,
don't remind me.

Let me have these views, the sun
so warm on my eyelids.

Something to laugh at

If there is no
peace in
my life,

I can
at least
laugh
at the chaos.

Being alive

There's a slight difference
between being awake
and being alive.

Being awake my eyes are open.
My body is in motion.
I'm breathing.

But being alive, I'm taking advantage-
absorbing the colors, I see
with my eyes.
Running freely until my chest burns.
Feeling others happiness and pain with them,
giving my tears freely.

Just because I'm awake,
certainly, doesn't mean
I'm living.

Tornados of Gossip

Sometimes I'm
stuck in the middle of a tornado.

Stuck in the "he said, she said" spiral.
Stuck in the "did you hear" and "can you believe" whirls.

I keep thinking I'll eventually
get thrown out of this tornado
and land on solid ground.
I'll be able to sit and watch
this tornado of gossip
leave and go to another field,
while I sit peacefully on my land
finally rid of the spinning and swirling.

That day never seems to come

I'm dizzy
from the
whiplash.
I'm dizzy
from the
noise.

Am I stuck because I don't know how to
let go and ride these violent winds?
Or because I don't think I'm strong
enough to throw myself out?

Burdens

I heard
there was another
school shooting
today.

I look down
holding my pile of laundry-
once a burden to me.

Now a soft place
to catch
my fallen tears.

Mom

In childhood there were very few things
that felt as safe and consistent,
secure and comforting,
soothing and centered,
as to walk through the front door
every day after school
hearing my mom call out to me,

I'm in here.

Dad

His jokes
were the backbone
to my childhood.
His attention
was the confidence
of my teen hood.
His tights hugs
are the warmth
in my adulthood.

Divorce

Looking into these two caskets
open and full.
Two bodies lying lifeless
expressionless and dull.

Vulnerable and exposed
to all the passersby.
Never making eye contact
to all those staring eyes.

"Did you hear what happened?"
They say, to every ear.
Not noticing the children
who are standing right there.

"Did she lose her mind?"
They'll say with disgust.
"Did he know that she was someone
That he couldn't trust?"

The gossip in tidal waves
ruining pride to be had.
Another story to them,
someone else's mom and dad.

As the kids stand around
these open caskets, with tears
thinking back to their lives
thinking back to all the years.

Years with open hope.
Years stable and kind.
Years with a mom and dad
our team who redefined.

They can't comprehend
their parents' marriage is dead.
The future so unknown,
all security shed.

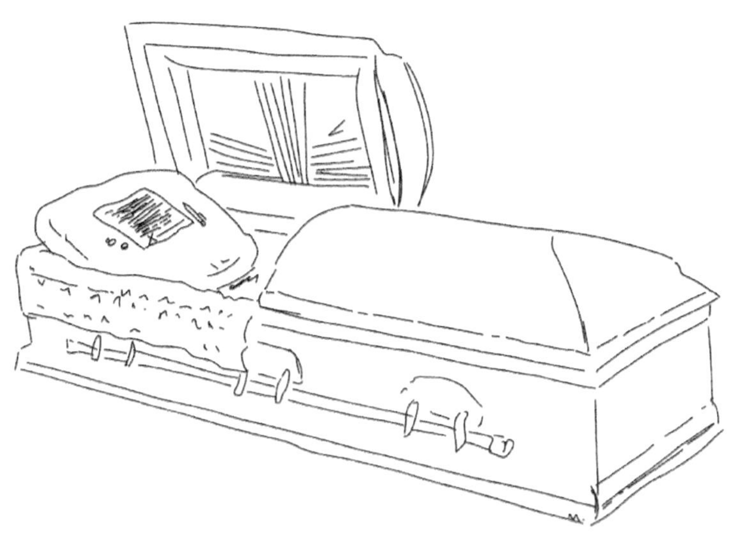

If only these types of deaths
were viewed as the real thing.
Flowers lining the sidewalks,
dinners inspired to bring.

If only people could see
that divorce is a death inside.
Our lives still in motion,
the foundation is what died.

What remains with us
are tender hearts survived.
Empathy engraved deep in the bones
for those who are still alive.

Easy fix

There's no greater
place
to rest
a troubled heart
then in the escapes
of a good book.

What is betrayal?

Is it ego?
Is it heartache?

What causes the sting?
Why in the moment,
Does it feel made for me?

How do I let go?
Does it burrow under my skin?
Does it find a home in my mind?

Is it possible to move on?
When the damage is done.
When I'm left feeling bitter
And patience is all gone?

What is anger?

> What causes the pain?
> Is it rooted in my body?
> Is it living in my mind?
>
> Why does it hurt?
> Does it start with pride?
> Or end with it?

Let go

There is so much
more room
for life,

by simply
letting go.

Dawn

The Sun has barely woken up-
she's quiet and calm.
Almost too calm.
She knows the world is still needing
it's sleep.

I step outside
to join her,
to breath in her air.
So crisp.
So delicious.

This is my coffee,
what she kindly provides.

I feel my heart start to beat.
I feel ready to start this day.

Open road

Who built these roads
Smooth and so black
Letting me drive
Without looking back

Who carved a road
In these thick, tall trees
I could stand in their midst
And feel this quiet peace

Who dusted this sand
In this dessert so dry
With the cactus so tall
Ever endless blue sky

Who used their hands
To chip at these roads
Straight to the ocean cliffs
Where time is slowed

Who used their strength
their precious time
To make these roads
That feel like mine

They curve to the top
At this mountain grand
Where I can see the world
Right where I stand

They bring me to places
I only see in my dreams
These endless smooth roads
These manmade streams

Dancing on Mountain Tops

We hiked to the top
not a soul was in sight.
So, we hit the "play" button
dancing into the night.

We danced for friendship
for life and for fun
we danced to remind us
we are still young.

We danced to the views
all its twinkling lights.
We danced to let go
all the daily fights.

We felt so alive
in that brisk, mountain air
so close to the stars
without a single care.

Mountain air

The air really is different.

Fresh and smooth.
No wonder these flowers
ache to come alive.

I breathe it deep.

Cleansing the toxic inside me.
Lifting the load off my spirit.
Drowning my negative thoughts-
invigorating my tired mind.

Purifying me from the inside.

I see the majesty around me-
the simple beauty in the details.
No judgement or critique.

Coaxing it back with me to the city.

I exhale all that I want to leave behind
and whisper "thank you" into the wind.

For the air
really is different up here.

God is a gardener

We head down South
to chase the sun,
and walk the desert sand.

We hike the trails
climb the rocks,
it's a hot and barren land.

With no water to be seen,
no vegetation around,
I wonder how anything grows.

In that moment I see
ahead on the trail,
a little color that shows.

I walk up to it,
there at my feet,
are purples, pinks and blues.

The prettiest flowers
I've ever seen,
growing down in the cracks by my shoes.

I wonder how this
could possibly be,
with no rain or rivers that flow.

And then I smile,
thinking of God,
for only He, the Gardner, knows.

Spring

I feel very similar
to Spring
you know.

Reaching as hard as I can
to pull my head
out
of the dirt-
to feel the sun
on my face.

Hoping for life, again
after a long
cold winter.

Summer

The windows are all open,
the sun wakes us up.
No plans for the day,
no schedule or makeup.

We put on our swimsuits
and grab our friends.
We head for the water,
until the day ends.

They swim in the lake
they dig in the sand,
they catch the minnows,
their cheeks so tan.

They stop to eat oranges,
and peel them fast.
Juice drips down their chins,
it reminds me of my past.

I was young like them,
before real life began.
Time didn't exist,
I spent hours in the sand.

It makes me smile,
watching time travel.
Being with them,
as childhood unravels.

These are the days,
they will look back on,
with nothing but play,
from dusk until dawn.

This is summer.
This is being a child.
This is living,
Free, happy, and wild.

Believing

To catch a firefly
and watch it glow
in your hands,
reopens the part of your brain
that once held the magic
believing unicorns run wild,
smiles not needing to be
earned, fairies fly in the forest-
rainbows still hold
pots of gold.

Fall

I look out the window
see the trees sway.
The cool northern breeze
is calling me by name.

I open the door,
feel autumn on my face.
It's cold. It's awakening.
It's delicious to the taste.

I hear leaves crunch
I see the colors turn
to orange, yellow,
reds that burn.

I throw on my wool sweater,
step through the door-
I need to be outside,
it's what Fall is for.

East Coast Seasons

Spring is
renewal

Fall is
religion

Winter mornings

It's 5:30 am
she's already up.
I'm half asleep
while I pick her up.

It's snowing quietly outside
still pitch black.
I make myself some tea
and lay her in my lap.

I wrap the blanket around her
throw the match to light the fire.
Whoever wakes up this early
I can't help but admire.

I nuzzle in next to her
tired as can be.
She points to a book,
her favorite one, I see.

I go over and grab it,
hoping she'll start to drift,
but as I read aloud
her mood starts to shift.

She perks right up,
her story being read.
All I can think about
is going back to bed.

She leans into my side,
wrapping her arm around my chest.
I look at the falling snow,
I doubt I need more rest.

Reading to her
by this fire feels so cozy.
I guess there are perks
to waking up this early.

To the man with little words

Dear man with little words,
smiles all the same.

Your spirit always high,
always up to play the game.

You show up when asked,
do more to please, than say.

For there is no need to chat,
when your actions are what stay.

Marriage

Why, yes
you can
have
all of me.

Only if you
allow me to change
everything about
myself.

Fighting

I once believed
the fights
creating the most damage
were the dramatic Broadway shows-
slamming doors,
screaming,
yelling,
and crying.

I understand now -
the sea of deep silence
is where the heart
slowly stops
beating.

Boomerang love

It took
me getting
away

to feel
closer
to you.

Getting away

We plan a trip,
To get away from them.
To talk and cuddle,
Finally sleep in.

We eat out,
We play around.
We watch movies
We hit the town.

But after a while,
Doing what we want
We start to notice,
While eating our croissant-

Once the thrill
Being alone has past,
Our minds drift to our girls
We want to get home fast.

We think how lonely
Our lives would be,
Without our children
We wouldn't see

How much happiness
We get from being Mom and Dad
How much joy
There is to be had.

As we walk the streets,
We find a window glass
Seeing our reflection
Both of us staring back.

We see a smiling couple
with no kids to be seen

Looking relaxed and free
Dressed up nice and clean

And we feel happy for them,
But deep down we know
That real happiness isn't here,
They're waiting for us at home.

Right before I run naked into the ocean with my husband

I want to seize
every moment
awaking my soul,
reminding me
I'm still alive-
amidst sleep walking
through endless
daily routines.

Forest floor for a good date

The rain was light on the leaves,
the drops remarkably therapeutic.
Moss was thick and soft,
better than a duvet
in my humble opinion.
Fog absorbing the fresh rain-
euphoria taking over.
The tree trunk, strong and sturdy,
the headboard was needed.
My hair dripping wet-
breath heavy.

Quietly yours

We live in a world
where the louder the love
the deeper its matter.

But in this small room,
just me and you–
I'm quietly yours.

Sunday mornings

In your arms
I want to stay
Time won't know
To start the day

Laying still
You can feel me breathe
Please don't leave
Please stay

.

FOMO

How do I live a life
where when I die,
I don't miss a thing?

Where I've lived it fully,
everything is satisfied?

Every part of me has been filled.

Every relationship has been full.
Every part of my body has been touched.
Every choice has been embraced.
Every talent has been edified.
Every word has been said.
Every meal has been loved.
Every moment has been savored.

How do I live a life
without the fear
of missing out?

Is it mundane?

Is it really so mundane,
the very foundation
to our life's
existence?

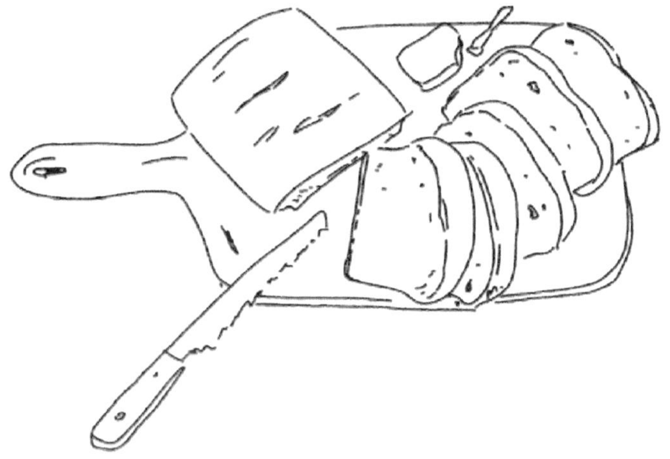

To life

To the stressed,
it is a long life.
To the happy,
it is a short life.
To the content,
it is a simple life.
To the busy,
it is a slaved life.
But to the grateful,

it is a beautiful life.

Life after a death

The beautiful peony
who worked so hard
to shine so brightly in life-
with its colors and smells,

cut down,
handled,
placed freshly
in a watered vase

for everyone
to admire
still.

Goodbyes

I don't cry for the pain
or for the loss.
I don't cry for the "never agains"
the "last times".
For the "I wish we could haves"
the "we didn't do's".

I cry for the joy
to have had you.

Love evident every day.
Forgiving hearts that were opened.
Kindnesses shared.
Hugs that held.
Teary laughs,
the ache to be together.

I cry for the love.
The abundance of love.

Melissa Elder lives on the east coast in Jersey with her husband and 2 girls amongst the trees. When she isn't capturing feelings through words, she is trying to capture them through a lens. *The Mundane* is her first book.

Acknowledgments

It's hard to believe in yourself, so for someone, anyone, to believe in you, is everything. Thank you, Mom and Dad. I can't believe I got so lucky to have two parents who didn't care about failure. You both simply wanted me to pursue my passion. Your daily encouragements and kind support shaped my courage and gave me the guts.

K.J., you are now family. Editing, publishing and encouraging me has now made you a part of my family. Whether you like it or not. Thank you for everything.

Achsa, you breathed life into this book with your designs and patience. Thank you for caring with me.

Maria, I'll never be able to fully thank you for your art that changed the entire feel of this book. I refuse to write a book without you.

Brad, you believed in me. In my heart, that's all that should be required for a gentle love. Thank you, my love.

My girls, how I love you-you have made my life anything but mundane.